BwB

This book [belongs to]
Louise Lommel
Aug 24, 2004
Love –
Joe & LaVonne

S0-BTE-024

This book is dedicated to the Minnesota farm families
who have persevered through the hard times
and are still doing what they love.

BwB

*"Our passion for farming is deep within our hearts...
the good life is here!"*

Donna Engles, Lake Crystal

LIFE ON THE FARM

A Pictorial Journey of Minnesota's Farmland and its People

Photography by
DEAN A. RIGGOTT

DEAN RIGGOTT PHOTOGRAPHY
ROCHESTER, MINNESOTA

Credits:

Photography: Dean Riggott

Design & Layout: Dean Riggott, Greg & Jodi Latza

Foreword: Brent Olson

Editing: Aleta Capelle & Mike Dougherty

Printing: Doosan Printing, Seoul, Korea

ISBN # 0-9659875-2-3

First edition / Soft cover / $ 24.95

Library of Congress Catalog Card # 00-111519

All rights reserved. No part of this publication may be reproduced or used in any form by any means - graphic, electronic, or mechanical, including framing, photocopying, recording, taping, nor any information storage and retrieval system - without prior written permission from the publisher

Copyright © 2001 Dean Riggott Photography

Published by: Dean Riggott Photography
831 10 1/2 Street S.W.
Rochester, MN 55902
Phone: 507-285-5076

www.riggottphoto.com
riggottphoto@home.com

Acknowledgements:

I would like to thank the following people for their help, support and cooperation:

My father, Don Riggott, who inspired me to become a photographer and for the support and guidance he has given me throughout my life and my career.

Kelly Boldan and Chris Frye, formerly of *Agri News*, who hired me to shoot for their publication. It opened my eyes to the beauty of the land and its people.

Greg Latza, whose book, *Back on the Farm*, was a true inspiration and whose support and friendship have been invaluable to my career.

And especially to the people in this book, who opened their doors to a stranger, and in turn have given us a glimpse into their lives and *Life on the Farm*.

"This is the best place to live in the whole world."

Sumner S. Sheldon, Houston

FOREWORD by Brent Olson

The images in this book have taken the better part of four years to compile but in many ways Dean Riggott has been preparing this book his entire life.

Dean's technical competence is impressive, but his hard won ability to reach into the heart of a scene and capture its essence is what sets his work apart from the rest. After all, this isn't a simple story to tell. When the glaciers finally departed for good 10,000 years ago, they left behind a landscape scoured and changed forever. From the stark Red River Valley in the northwest where the only hills are made of sugar beets to the bluffs, hills, and streams of southeastern Minnesota, we have a state full of geographical contrasts. Dean has spent many years traveling the highways and byways of rural Minnesota. People traveling from New York to Los Angeles may consider the Midwest fly-over land, but a purely local example of that same mentality could be called Interstate blinders. There's a lot more to Minnesota than the vistas you can see from the rest stops and gas stations lining the highways. Dean has driven many miles on the back roads capturing images of a landscape never seen by many travelers. But in truth, the variety of our landscapes pale in comparison to the contrasts among our people. You'll see that many of Dean's photos show an overpowering landscape where the people are few and scattered. Still, despite that physical separation and isolation, people who live in the country prize their sense of community above all else. The philosopher Sam Keen has written that when he gives workshops on personal mythology he always asks people to draw a picture of where they would like to live. Ninety-five percent of the time the pictures are of a rural area. What draws us so strongly to the country, while more and more of us leave as fast as we can? How can a community flourish where miles between neighbors are a common thing? And how does such a cold, harsh, climate breed such warm and friendly people?

The first time I met Dean Riggott, I was working on a story for *Successful Farming*. In my capacity as a farmer willing to endure public humiliation I had agreed to install and learn to use a yield monitor despite a profound ignorance of the entire procedure. Dean was supposed to document my struggles. He arrived on time at Lund Implement, in Madison. I knew immediately that he was the photographer because he wasn't wearing any socks and he was carrying a load of gear that would fell a pack mule.

I was a little concerned. I knew nothing of Dean, and I was fairly confident that spending a day taking pictures of a farmer working on a combine was not near the top of the list of anyone's desirable activities. Little did I know that Dean spends a great deal of time doing exactly that, and of his own free will besides.

As good photographers do, Dean soon disappeared to me as I went about my portion of the story. I crawled in and around my combine, puzzled over the installation manual and tried not to drill holes in anything important. There would be an occasional burst of light from a strobe and a very occasional instruction or request, but it wasn't until I reviewed some of Dean's photos that I became aware of his creative and technical excellence. I am pleased and honored to write this foreword for his new book.

You should cherish this book. Cherish it for the quality of the pictures and for the captions that serve to deepen your understanding of the scenes portrayed. For instance, the photo of a smiling Donna Engles, standing in a field of soybeans while out picking weeds with her family, does suggest a person at ease with her place in the world, but for a deeper understanding, it helps to have her own words. "We love the dirt, the smell of dirt and playing in the dirt," said Donna Engles. "Our passion for farming is deep within our hearts ... the good life is here!"

In the same vein, the photo of an old man climbing a ladder into a wooden granary is visually stunning, but when you read the caption you find out that rather than just being an anonymous photographer's subject you have here a man named Merrill Gustafson, who moved to this farm in 1950 from another farm just a couple miles down the road. Why did he move?

"I guess it's the Gypsy in me", said Merrill.

That's something a lot of books about rural Minnesota miss. They cover the hard - working, honest, God-fearing part pretty well but they miss completely that our people are funny! They have to be. Grim determination might get you through a crisis, but it won't get you through seventy or eighty years of flood, drought, or hailstorms. For that you need a sense of humor and the ability to step back and laugh when a truly rational person would collapse in a pool of tears. From Gayle and Marlin Timms' morning dance recital at 6 a.m. outside the door of their dairy barn to Donna Engles' conversion of work boots into flowerpots, there is a pervasive spirit of quiet good humor.

Roots grow better in dirt than in concrete. That's a fact of nature. The great writer Flannery O'Connor once left her hometown and traveled to New York for some literary event. That night she attended a party in her honor and listened in bewilderment to the clever conversation of the intellectuals in attendance. Later in the evening she exploded "These people aren't from anywhere!"

We always know where we're from. The old hometown holds our affections with a strength that doesn't seem to waver, no matter how far away we stray. Even in these days of double or triple hyphen schools, reunions are still big summertime business and there is an ever increasing stream of people retiring back to the small towns they grew up in, drawn by inexpensive housing, helpful neighbors, and a level of peace and tranquility that is impossible to find amongst big buildings or the wilderness of suburbia.

And, of course, some of us never leave. On the cover of this book is a shot of John Bauer absorbing the warmth of an afternoon sun while his brother harvests soybeans. John has been farming since he started helping with chores in 1923. When asked about retirement, John says, "I suppose I'll have to eventually, but I'm not looking forward to it." I know many farmers like John and knowing them has made me sanguine about any future unemployment problems here in the country. The simple fact is that when all these men who grew up on farms during the Depression pass from the scene it will take two or three regular workers to replace them. They live in a world where being called a good worker is the ultimate accolade and old men keep working, through bad hips and cancer surgeries, because working is what they know, and the pleasures of seeing another crop come in far outweighs the pain of getting out of bed one more morning. For what they realize is that, no matter what else happens in rural areas, farmers grow food for hungry people and it's hard to imagine a more validating line of work to be in. When I combine wheat, on an average day in average wheat, I harvest enough in an hour to make 20,000 loaves of bread. Perhaps it is whimsy on my part, but at the end of a long day I take great pleasure in thinking of how many tables will be set with bread that had its beginnings on my farm.

Having the long perspective is not always comforting. Dean photographed Sumner S. Sheldon. Mr. Sheldon, then 87 years old, shared his views of farm life in the final months of his life. Sheldon operated the rural Houston farm that had been owned by his father, who had taken it over from his father.

In his later years, Sheldon napped daily in the very room where he was born in 1911. "I've seen a lot of change in my time and I don't think it's all for the better," said Sheldon while reflecting on his years as a farmer.

Yet, he had no regrets in his choice of where to spend his days.

" This is the best place to live in the whole world," Sheldon told a photographer as he gazed out the kitchen window of his rural Houston farm.

Times are changing with astonishing rapidity. In 1950 my county had 10,000 people in it. Now there are less than 5,000. But that is nothing new. Things always change. The Lakota and the Chippewa found that out when their lands were swarmed by hungry, eager, immigrants anxious for some land of their own. The Bonanza farmers of the Red River Valley found it out also in the 1880s. They thought they had established a new era of agriculture and they were all gone in less than twenty years.

In the 1980s, we were told to farm fencerow to fencerow, because a hungry world would buy all the food we could ever raise. Now India and China export food and we struggle to maintain the markets we do have.

There is no denying we live in complicated times. Low prices, genetic modifications, bigger farms, smaller schools: each contribute to a sense of uneasiness. Sometimes it can be hard to find a common ground. It's easy to look at rural Minnesota as a place of extremes. Hard-charging young businessmen farming thousands of acres with a boost from major corporations and old people hanging on to a vanished way of life. The truth is a lot more complicated. It takes more than the two ends of the spectrum to describe a rainbow. The extremes are there, but there are also young boys daydreaming about driving tractors and contented couples happily raising their children in a time and a place they have chosen as the best for their families.

Through it all, the people of rural Minnesota have gotten up early, worked late, raised their families and built a way of life that cherishes both independence and interdependence. Everyone is expected to pull their own weight, but when trouble does strike, no one gathers as quickly to take up the slack, be it hot dishes after a death in the family or several million dollars in equipment to help harvest a neighbor's crop.

As you turn the pages in this book, you will see the old and the young, the past and the future, hope and despair, and through it all, love and vitality. You will see resiliency and endurance.

As a storyteller myself, I know it can be very easy to simply weave a tale. It is infinitely harder to tell the truth. Dean Riggott has done both.

Brent Olson is uniquely suited to writing the foreword for this book. Descended from hundreds of years of peasants working the land, Brent and his wife Robin live on the Ortonville farm his grandparents homesteaded 120 years ago. He farms 1,200 acres of corn, wheat, and soybeans. His weekly column, *Independently Speaking*, is carried by publications across the country. Brent is also the author of two books, *The Lay of the Land*, and *Letters From a Peasant*.

Luverne Theel, Eyota

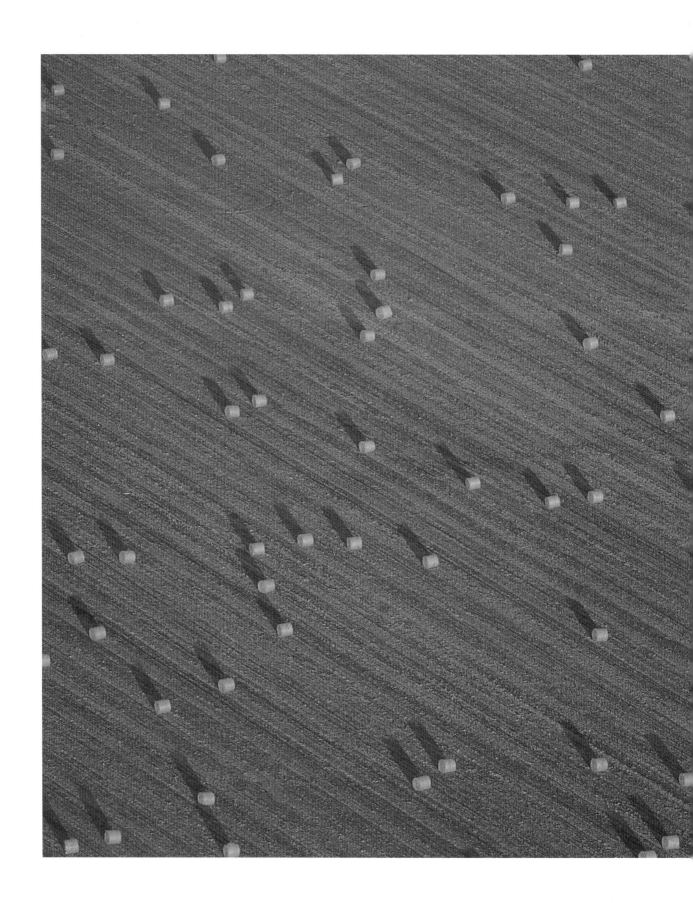

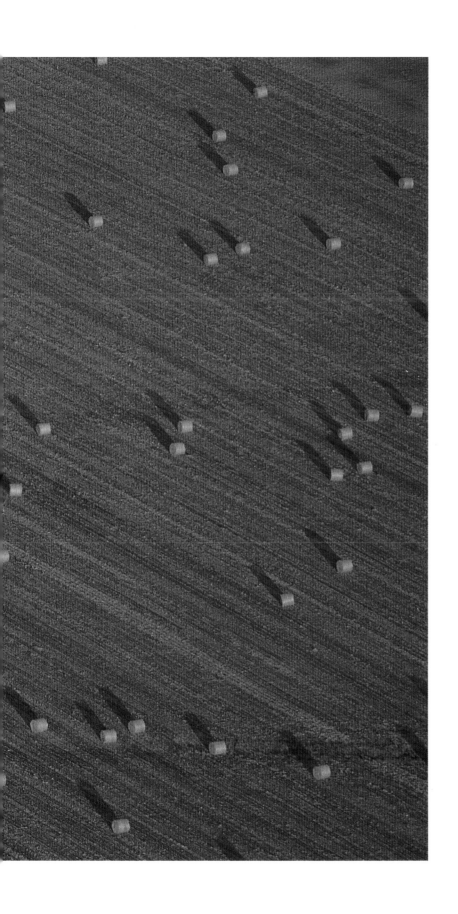

Round Bales

Large round bales cast long shadows across a field in southeastern Minnesota. Farmers secure a variety of crops and crop bi-products into large round and square bales for various uses on and off the farm. State statistics show six of the 10 top counties in hay production are located in southeastern Minnesota. They are Fillmore (third); Winona (fifth); Goodhue (sixth); Houston (eighth); Wabasha (ninth) and Olmsted (10th).

Spring Planting

LeRoy Bertran fills his planter with fertilizer as the setting sun colors the sky. Five-o-clock does not mark the end of the workday for farmers as they must take advantage of good weather when the planting season arrives. LeRoy was planting corn on the land he and his two brothers, Donald and Ralph, farm in Zoin Township near Roscoe. "We've been here all our lives," said LeRoy. His parents, Leo and Sarah Bertran, raised 10 children on the farm, which they homesteaded in 1936. Nine of the 10 children are still farming in the area.

Three Little Lambs

Three, week-old lambs, curiously eye a visitor to Gretchen and Kip Meredith's sheep farm near Rochester. The couple grew up in the city, however Kip spent time on a relative's farm as a child. "I've always enjoyed working with livestock. Especially in the spring when they're lambing," said Kip. The Merediths have raised sheep since 1987. Their 185 ewes give birth each spring to a like number of lambs. Besides yielding an annual crop of wool, lambs are sold or kept as replacement ewes by Minnesota sheep farmers.

Wishful Thinking

"This is what we do at the elevator -- wish we were fishing," joked Brian Sylskar as he strung a small, pink fishing rod for his 5-year-old daughter, Blair, during a slow time in late June at the Hoffman Co-Op Grain Association in Hoffman. Brian was planning to take Blair, his wife, Carol, and son Landon, 9, fishing for panfish at an area lake that evening. "I wish I were good enough to do it for a living," said Brian of the pastime he has enjoyed since he was a small boy. Brian has worked at the co-op since 1989.

Workin' the Phones

Tim Bolgrean works the phones buying and marketing grain in his office at the Hoffman Co-Op Grain Association in Hoffman. Bolgrean started working at an elevator in his hometown of Barnsville at age 18, then moved to Hoffman in 1980 to manage that elevator. "I guess I'd have to say it's the people" said Tim, when asked what he likes best about the job.

God's Country

A bird's-eye view shows miles of rolling hills during harvest season in south-eastern Minnesota. For hundreds of thousands of years, glaciers crossed and recrossed the land now called Minnesota leaving gently rolling hills. Only a few areas, including a small section of land in the southeast corner of the state, were untouched by glacial activity.

Sowing the Seeds

LeRoy Bertran steers a 1960 Oliver 660 while planting corn on the land he and his two brothers, Donald and Ralph, farm near Roscoe in Stearns County. "We've got a lot of use out of it," said Bertran of the tractor the brothers bought in 1965. As for his life as a farmer, Bertran responds, "I got no complaints about it.... You just gotta make the best of it from day to day. You keep at it, and keep at it, and after a while you don't know any better."

Quite a Collection

Don Dahlstrom drives a 1946 John
Deere LI down Main Street during the
annual Foley Fun Days parade in
Benton County. Behind that is a 1951
MI, and a 1941 BR, all belonging to
Ken Monroe of Foley, who has been
collecting the old tractors for 13 years.
Monroe's interest in tractors started
when he was young and he began
collecting toy tractors. While his big
tractor collection numbers 35, his
toy collection has swelled to more
than 400.

End of a Day

The sun sets over the Roger Eicken farm near Black Hammer in Houston County. Eicken's parents, Norman and Doris, bought the farm in 1945. Since retiring in 1995, Eicken has rented out the land he once farmed with his two sons, Ashley and Richard. "I loved it, but it just didn't pay," Eicken said. His sons have since found work in the city.

"Old Guys"

George Glieden, left, chats with Willard Volker during an auction near Dalton. "I know all these old guys," said Glieden, who has been retired from farming since 1976. He said he attends auctions to buy and resell and visit with the "old guys." Glieden grew up near Belgrade and farmed there all his life. Volker had another explanation for being at the sale: "I just came to the auction to kill time." Volker grew up and farmed near Elbow Lake until his retirement in 1979, but said he doesn't believe in the adage "You can't take it with you." Said Volker of his farm: "It's just layin' there and I'm gonna take it along."

Workin' Out

Mark Revier, 12, and his border collie, Cody, condition 4-H lambs on the family farm near Olivia in Renville County. A wagon pulled by an all-terrain vehicle works the animals hind quarters. Mark planned to show the market wether lambs at the county fair and hoped to go on to the Minnesota State Fair in Falcon Heights. The Revier Feedlot, which is owned by Mark's grandparents, Gene and Erma, and his parents, Tami and Jeff, raises 5,000 head of beef cattle and 1,700 acres of corn and soybeans.

Winter Feed

Charles Wendt pulls into the
Stewartville All-American Co-Op on a
brisk winter morning to buy a load of
corn for his herd of dairy and beef
cows. Wendt farms with his brother,
Dave, and with help from his daughter,
Melissa. Dave lives on the farm his
grandfather, Albert Wendt, homesteaded
in 1890. Charles is just down the road.
"It has its ups and downs but it's a
good way of life," said Charles on his
life as a farmer. "It's a great way and
place to raise a family."

Standing Guard

A lone, fog-shrouded tree stands guard among fields of corn, alfalfa and soybeans near Whalan in Fillmore County. Very much a part of the Corn Belt, Minnesota has some of the most fertile land in the nation. Corn remains one of the state's biggest cash crops.

Handy Helpers

Kayla Serbus, 10, her sister Desiree, 8, and cousins Samantha, 9, and Mitchell, 6, help pick up field stones on a summer evening near Olivia in Renville County. Kayla and Desiree's dad, Kirt Serbus (on tractor), grew up on a farm just a half mile down the road. Now he farms with brothers Todd, Galen, and father Richard, raising corn, soybeans, and cattle. Besides picking up rocks, Kayla and Desiree help around the farm by taking care of a Shetland pony they were given by Santa Claus.

Bindin' Corn

Amish farmer Adin Shetlar, 20, binds corn with a corn-binder pulled by three Belgian horses as the setting sun lights up the sky on a warm September evening. Shetlar farms with his parents, five brothers and a sister near Utica. "I like farming O.K.," said Shetlar, "but I'd like to become a carpenter."

Potato Harvest

George Cariveau harvests potatoes on the family farm in East Grand Forks. George's father, Duane, started growing potatoes in 1962 and George has been helping since he was a kid. "I used to sleep in the back of the tractor window...I spent hours out there with him," said George. The Cariveaus grow 200 to 400 acres each year and sell the potatoes through Ryan Potato Company in East Grand Forks. Minnesota ranks seventh in potato production in the United States.

Forage Expo

Adam Goeden, left, and his uncle, Kevin Goeden, listen in on an alfalfa cutting demonstration at the Eighth Annual Minnesota Alfalfa and Forage Expo at the West Central Research and Outreach Center at the University of Minnesota, Morris campus. The Goedens raise 50 head of dairy, and 640 acres of crops, including canola, on their farm in Wadena. The annual event gives attending farmers a look at the latest in equipment and technology and a chance to learn more about the industry.

Bagging it Up

Earl Zenzen has worked for the
Belgrade Milling Company for more
than 20 years. Here, the Belgrade
native loads freshly packed bags of
calf feed onto a dolly to be stored in
the company's warehouse. The feed
company, which is owned by Al Beste,
has been doing business for more than
100 years.

One Big Move

Merrill Gustafson climbs a ladder
against an old corn crib on the Stanton
farm he and his brother Bud started
farming in 1950. Before taking over the
farm, the two lived just a mile down the
road. Why did they move? "I guess it's
the Gypsy in me," Gustafson joked.
Gustafson's son-in-law, Al Kieffer,
operates the farm now that Merrill and
Bud have retired.

Front Row Seat

Clyde Larson waits in the shade as he fills a wagon with soybeans headed for the local co-op. Larson, who raises 2,000 hogs as well as crops, grew up farming with his father, Wallace, on a nearby Hanska farm. Larson has been helping on the farm since he can remember but wasn't always sure that he would become a farmer. After attending college in Mankato, he decided to return to the family farm. "I like being my own boss and working outside," said Larson.

Homeward Bound

An Amish buggy makes its way down a country road near the tiny town of Black Hammer in Fillmore County. The Amish community is very private yet prominent in southeastern Minnesota. One will often pass a horse-drawn buggy on the country roads.

Age Brings Wisdom

Born in Iowa in 1914, Leonard Voigt has farmed all his life, living in Preston since 1958 where he raises crops, beef cows, and horses, with his wife Ruby and son Rick. Why hasn't Leonard retired? Ruby has the explanation: "He's done it for so many years, it's hard to quit. He's always liked to work." Voigt farmed with horses until just a couple of years ago, using the Percherons to plant and spread manure. He still uses an old corn picker for the few acres he farms. Would they do it all again? Ruby answers: "Oh yes, farming is all we ever knew. But unfortunately I think it's changed for the worse."

Takin' a Break

Ben Frieler, 6, and his 24-year-old horse, Nugget, take a break while riding with his sister, Pam, 15, in Swanville. Pam and her 11-year-old quarter horse, Tanya, compete in weekly horse shows in the Western Pleasure Class. Ben hopes to compete one day with Nugget. Their father, Fred, is a cattle dealer and their mother, Sandy, works as a clerk at a sale barn. The family also raises crops on their Swanville farm.

Fresh Eggs

Zachary and Megan Riggott leave the chicken coop with their mother, Kathy, and a basket of freshly laid eggs on their hobby farm in Afton, Dakota County. The Riggotts enjoy life on the farm even though they rent their land to neighboring farmers. The family is not alone in living on a farm but making their living elsewhere. As more and more acres are needed to make a living off the land, one-time city-dwellers are moving into the farmsteads that become available as the land is swallowed up into neighboring farms either through rental agreements or purchases.

Rush Hour

The sun starts to set while Bob Hain waits in line with a load of soybeans at the Stewartville All-American Co-Op. Hain has worked for Robert Vaupel in Stewartville, harvesting and hauling grain part-time since renting out his farm in the 1980s. Hain spent 41 years working for AMPI Dairy in Rochester and running his farm but it "got to be too much. It's hard to give it up, especially when you were born on a farm," said Hain.

Bird's-Eye View

A farmer pilots a combine through a
stand of corn in southeastern
Minnesota. Field corn is grown in the
United States on more acres than any
other crop. Field corn is grown for
animal feed, silage and processing.
In 1998, nearly 6.8 million acres of
land were devoted to corn production.

Quite an Office

Mark Schwartz sits on the drawbar
of a gravity box wagon as his brother,
Bruce, combines corn on their Morris-
town land. The two were finishing up
90 acres of corn so they could harvest
55 acres of soybeans. Harvest season in
Minnesota is one of the best -- though
busiest -- times of the year for farmers.
Temperatures have given way to cooler
weather, however, shorter days make
for hectic times as the crops are
brought in for the year.

Drying Popcorn

Ears of popcorn dry on a clothesline on the porch of Sandi Hunter's home in rural Money Creek in Houston County. "This is the first time I've tried it," said Sandi, who grew the corn in her garden. "I got the idea from a friend and thought I'd try it."

Bernard's Treasures

Antiques, tools, and old machinery are auctioned off on the Pangerl farm near Pine City, Royalton Township. Bernard Pangerl made his living from milk cows and crops until the 1950s when he had to retire due to poor health. He died of heart disease in January 1999. "It was hard for all of us kids to see it go," said daughter Sherri Pangerl-Anderson. "This was one of the better sales ... everyone had fun," said auctioneer Kevin Norby, left. "That's the way their father would have wanted it."

A Loyal Friend

Richard Gullickson of rural Amherst in Fillmore County tills a field as his dog, Nellie, trails behind. Richard and his father, Gordon, plant 320 acres of crops on their farm that is also home to 50 head of beef cattle. The farm has been in the family since 1857, and the family's "Century Farm" plaque is prominently displayed on their garage. If the farm is to stay in the family it will be up to Richard's two sons, Adam and Eric.

Morning Dance

Marlin and Gayle Timm step outside their barn for a dance during their early-morning milk chores. The Plainview couple take dance lessons regularly and are often found practicing the steps they learned the night before. "Our feed consultant talked us into it," Gayle explained. "It's a real stress reliever." The Timms have farmed the Plainview land since the late-1800s when Marlin's great-great-grandfather, Albert, moved to the area from Germany and homesteaded a farm just two miles down the road.

Out to Dry

A pair of overalls hang on a post to
dry on a farm in southeast Minnesota.
Overalls are the uniform of choice for
most farmers. Besides protection from
the elements, they help reduce the
amount of laundry a farm wife has
to face by protecting the rest of the
farmer's clothes from dirt and grime
encountered every day in farm work.

The Last Kernel

Jeff Taylor, left, and Vic Bolstad empty
a truck-load of corn on a busy fall day at
the Stewartville All-American Co-Op.
"I like it here," Bolstad said. "They're
all good guys to work with." Bolstad
grew up on a farm in Sargeant, bought
his Stewartville farm in 1963, and
retired from farming in 1993. "I just got
old and tired," said Bolstad. Taylor grew
up in Stewartville and has worked for
the co-op since 1975.

First Auction

Five-year-old Kent Miller attends his first livestock auction with his father, Joe Miller, at the Belgrade Livestock Auction Market in Stearns County. The company, which is owned by Tom Schaefer, holds a livestock auction every Thursday afternoon selling cows, calves, bulls, pigs, sheep, horses, and goats. Kent got a chance to bid and bought a young calf, which he named "Cory", after his step-brother. "He just loves livestock," said his dad. The Millers raise dairy and crops on their farm near Marshall, which has been in the family since 1930.

This Little Piggy...

Mark Fishbaugher corrals pigs being auctioned at Harmony Livestock Sales in Harmony. The feeder pig auctions were once held every Tuesday but due to low hog prices and a lack of farmers raising the animals, the company closed its doors in 1995. "It just wasn't profitable for the small farmer to raise hogs," said Tye Eicken, an employee with Wiechman Pig Company that now operates out of the former auction house. The company buys pigs from the area and markets them around the country.

Junior Worker

"You're supposed to get dirty on a steam engine," said Henri Kieffer, 2 1/2, seen here playing on a 65-horse, half-scale Case steam tractor, at the 47th Western Minnesota Threshers Reunion in Rollag. Henri is the son of Ann Kieffer and Sven Biermann of Moorhead. The 1914 steam engine replica belongs to the Rev. Gregg Staudinger of Montana. Each year, close to 50,000 steam engine enthusiasts from around the country gather at the four-day Rollag reunion, which was started by the Nelson brothers in 1953 and is now run by more than 2,000 volunteers.

Row by Row

Daryl Bluhm cultivates corn on his rural Zumbro Falls farm where he and his twin brother, David, operate a dairy and crop farm. The two brothers took over the farm their parents, Cleo and Alona Bluhm, raised them on. "They made us go on to school and do other work first," said Daryl, who earned a degree in Ag Structure and Equipment. After working construction for a couple of years, he returned to the farm he calls home. "I've really enjoyed it," said Daryl.

Year After Year

"You can buy it but it just isn't the same," said Emma Hartwig, 92, as she worked in the garden she has planted yearly since 1930. Ms. Hartwig was born on a farm two miles down the road and has lived on her Swanville farm since 1930. She and her husband, William Hartwig, raised crops and dairy until he died in 1968. Emma now rents the land to her son-in-law, Gene Hadin.

Room Service

Thomas Evans feeds young Holstein calves a milk replacer on the farm his son and daughter-in-law, Paul and Carol Evans, have taken over in Culdrum Township near Little Falls. The Evanses milk cows and raise corn and alfalfa on the farm Thomas purchased in 1959. Paul took over the farm when his father retired in 1997, however Thomas still helps out with chores such as feeding and field work. "I'm the go-fer," says Thomas. "I go-fer this and go-fer that."

Fields and Feathers

A flock of birds glide over a cornfield in southeastern Minnesota just before harvest time. Corn is one of the major crops grown in southeastern Minnesota. Besides the market animals for which much of it is intended, field corn also provides food for the state's abundant wildlife.

Newborn Calves

A mother Holstein licks one of the twin calves she gave birth to just four hours earlier on a farm operated by Jim Kubasch and his son Gary near New Germany in Carver County. Jim and Gary tend 200 acres of crops as well as dairy and pigs on the farm that was started by Gary's great-grandparents, Charles and Emelia Kubasch, in the summer of 1900 just after they immigrated from Germany.

Rural Recess

Sam Hunter, 7, watches from the tree as his 8-year-old brother Cyrus swings from a rope swing at their rural Money Creek home in Houston County. The two were taking a recess from being home-schooled by their mother, Sandi. "If they're done with their math, they can have recess," said Sandi. As to why the children are home-schooled? "I believe the Lord led us to that," said Sandi.

Standing Tall

A field of sunflowers turn their faces toward the setting sun near Farmington in Dakota County. In Minnesota, the major field crops have been supplemented with such crops as sunflowers, potatoes, sugar beets, flax and vegetables. Minnesota ranks fifth in the nation in sunflower production, according to the National Agricultural Statistics Service.

"The Good Life"

"We love the dirt, the smell of dirt, and playing in the dirt," said Donna Engles, pictured here in a soybean field while out "walking a bean field" one beautiful summer evening with her husband John, sons Jay and Brian, and daughter, Lauren. "Our passion for farming is deep within our hearts... the good life is here!" Donna says she walked bean fields for money when she was a young girl living in the country just a few miles from the family farm in Lake Crystal, Blue Earth County.

Kickin' up Dust

The setting sun lights up the dust
kicked up during a soybean harvest
on a cool fall day in southeastern
Minnesota. According to the latest
estimates by the National Agricultural
Statistics Service, Minnesota ranks
third in the United States for soybean
production and fourth in corn production.

Workin' Hands

The hands of 76-year-old farmer Luverne Theel grasp the handle of a silage fork as he takes a break on his Eyota farm in Olmsted County. Despite two heart bypass surgeries and radiation therapy for cancer, Luverne is still going strong and has no plans to retire. "Not as long as I can get up and go," said Theel. "It's in my blood."

Window of Opportunity

Ken Krebs cultivates corn on a late summer evening on the farm he operates in Albany. Krebs raises crops, sheep, steers, chickens, and custom feeds cattle on the farm where he was born and raised. "I sleep in the room I was born in and I'll probably die there," says Krebs. On his life as a farmer Krebs replies, "I don't know that I'd do it again." The photo was taken through the window of an old cook shack, once used to cook meals for farmers on threshing crews in North Dakota.

Down Time

Down time at the auction is spent
sitting and waiting or grabbing a bite
to eat. It gave these two men from
Wisconsin time to do some figuring
on the back of an envelope while they
sat in the cafe of the Zumbrota
Livestock Auction. Tom and Gerry
Webster own the livestock auction
business, which has been in their family
for three generations. "It's been a really
good business for our family," says
Tom, who lives across the street on the
farm where he grew up.

Colorful Crop

Dennis Siegle cuts alfalfa on son
Steven's land near Cologne in Carver
County. The alfalfa will be stored as
silage and fed to 50 head of dairy and
young stock on Steven's farm. Steven
raises dairy cattle and crops and runs a
shop where he repairs farm machinery.
Dennis milked cows until 1992 and
now raises only crops on the farm he
has operated since 1954, just a few
miles down the road in Waconia.

Second to None

Erin Schnobrich, 18, leads
her red and white calf,
Jasmine, through the show
arena at the Brown County
Fair in New Ulm where they
took first place in their class.
Erin has been showing 4-H
animals since she was eleven
and made it to the State Fair
in 1997. She grew up with
four sisters and one brother
on the family's farm near
New Ulm, where her parents,
Rick and Kathy Schnobrich,
make their living from dairy
cows and crops.

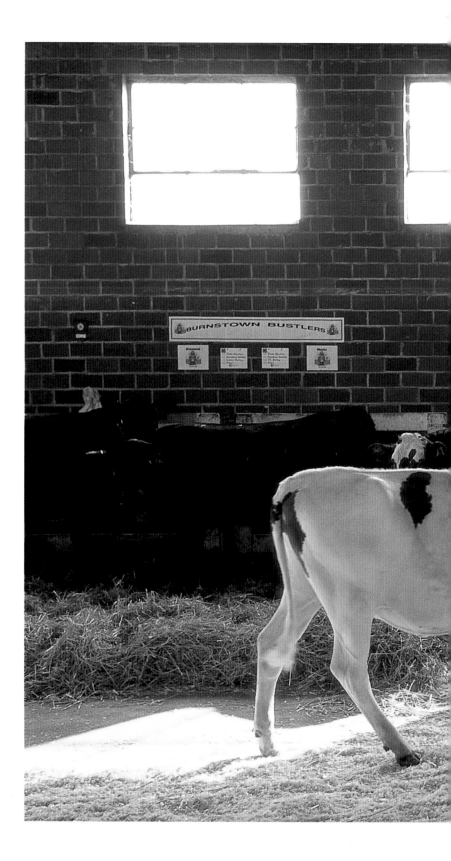

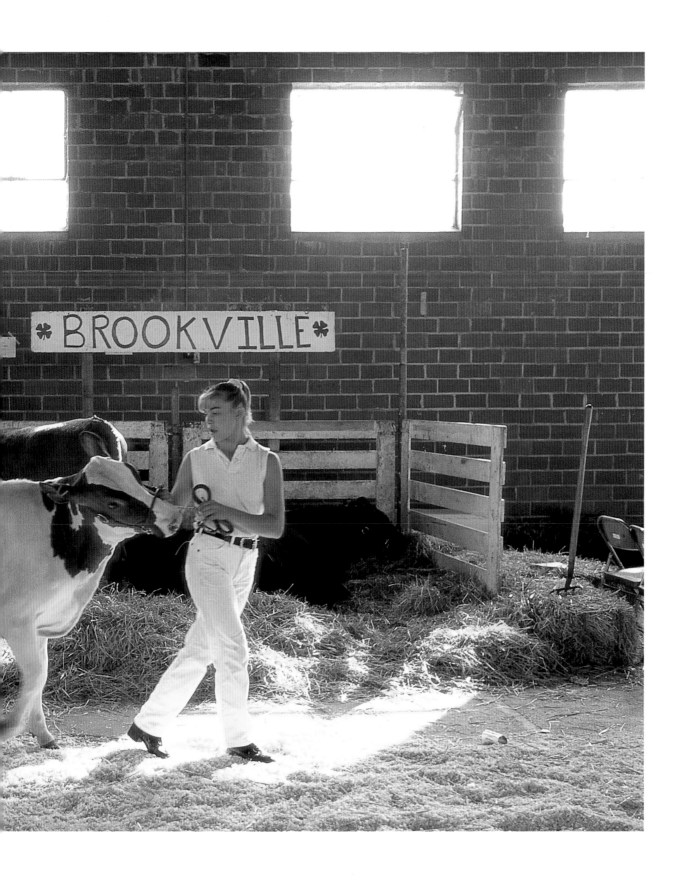

Spring Planting

Ron Fults fills a planter with seed corn on his farm near Sanborn, where he has farmed the land since 1960. Since injuring his hand in a combine in 1990, he has worked part-time. Fults is among farmers that helped place Minnesota fourth in the United States in corn production, according to recent federal estimates.

Move em' Out

Ray Rueter herds cattle into stalls at Central Livestock in Albany. The Albany auction barn is like auction barns throughout Minnesota that offer farmers a place to market livestock and gather with neighbors to discuss the farm economy. Minnesota ranks as one of the top meat-packing states, in part because its fertile ground has made corn a significant fattening grain for animals.

Sharing a Laugh

Andy Linaman, left, and Darwin Tri
share a laugh while waiting for the
next group of cattle in the alley at the
Zumbrota Livestock Auction in
Zumbrota. Tom and Gerry Webster
own the business that has been in their
family for three generations. "It's been
a really good business for our family,"
says Tom, who lives across the street
on the farm where he grew up. What's
the best part of the business? "The
people and the competition, it gets in
your blood. It's a lot of work and risk,
but we've been successful."

Solitary Sentry

An old F-14 Farmall tractor, likely
built during the Great Depression, is
silhouetted against the evening sky at
the Allen and Jennifer Whipple home
just north of Rochester. "It's sentimen-
tal," said Whipple, who has owned the
tractor since 1950. "It was my first
tractor. I bought it with extra money
I earned while working part-time at
Libby's Foods (in Rochester)."
Whipple was the youngest of twelve
children who grew up on the family
farm in Zumbro Falls, Wabasha
County.

"Farming for Fun"

"This is the best place to live in the whole world," said the late Sumner S. Sheldon, then 87 years old, as he looked out his kitchen window on the Houston farm, which was once owned by his grandfather. "I've seen a lot of change in my time and I don't think it's all for the better," said Sheldon while reflecting on his years as a farmer. But through all the changes, farming has been a good life. "Nobody's had a better life than I had." When asked why he still farms, Sheldon replied, "I'm farming for fun. There's no nicer job than to be sitting up in the combine when everything's working while combining corn or something."

Decorating the Sky

A sliver moon hangs like a decoration near this Minnesota windmill. Windmills, once vital to Minnesota farmers as a way to pump water for themselves and their animals, are becoming harder and harder to find. Most that do remain are no longer used.

A New Season

A baby robin, which was born in a nest above the front door, sits on a swinging bench in the back yard of the Pat and Deb Neville home in Spring Valley, Fillmore County. The first robin sightings of the season are taken by farmers as a sign that spring has arrived.

"Labor of Love"

George Cariveau harvests potatoes along with hired hand, Derrick Rasmussen, on the family farm in East Grand Forks. George's father, Duane, started growing potatoes in 1962 and George planted his first crop when he was just 18. "It's a labor of love. You're not gonna get rich doing it so you gotta love to do it," said George. "I get to watch a lot of sunrises and sunsets and if it rains I can go fishing." The Cariveaus grow 200 to 400 acres each year and sell the potatoes through Ryan Potato Company in East Grand Forks.

Milk Parlor

Joe Czech milks cows with son Mark on their farm near Foley in Benton County. The Czech family milks 200 cows and tends 2,100 acres of corn, soybeans, alfalfa, and small grains on the farm Joe bought in 1954. The farm started out with only 160 acres, seven dairy cows and the need for a lot of repairs. "He told me if I wanted to farm he'd marry me," Joe's wife Claudette recalls. "I cried when I saw the place," she said of the once shabby little farm.

Sitting Idle

Surrounded by snow, a 1020
McCormick-Deering tractor, circa
1936, sits idle in a field on the Chuck
Passe farm near Rochester in Olmsted
County. Passe, who works construction
and farms part-time, said the tractor
was in a shop fire in the late 1980s
and hasn't been used since. His parents,
Eugene and Francis, have scaled back
their operation to 60 acres and a dozen
beef cows on the farm they have owned
since 1949.

Sweepin' Up

Roy Blakstad sweeps up after unloading corn at the Goodhue Elevator Association's Wanamingo branch facility. The corn was later sent to Red Wing, where it was loaded onto barges and sent down the Mississippi River. About 18 percent of the corn grown in the United States is exported to other countries. The United States is the world's largest producer of corn, the world's largest exporter of corn and the world's largest consumer of corn.

Greener Pastures

Art Thicke leads his 85-cow dairy herd to a fresh pasture on his farm near LaCrescent in Houston County. Thicke is among a growing number of farmers going back to rotational grazing in an effort to preserve the land and cut costs. In 1987, Thicke divided his 84 acres of pasture into 42 two-acre paddocks. The cows are moved to a different paddock at least twice daily, allowing the pasture grasses to recover and the manure to be spread evenly across the land.

Right on Target

The sun sets between two trees near Choice and Black Hammer in Fillmore County. For many farmers, the setting of the sun doesn't mark the end of their work day. Planting and harvesting season mean longer hours in the field. Meanwhile, the needs of farm animals continue even when farmers are tending the crops. Yet, despite the hours, it's a life most farmers wouldn't trade for any other.

Dinner is Served

Cats and kittens get their daily feeding of fresh milk on the Marlin and Gayle Timm farm near Plainview. Cats can be found on most Minnesota farms, especially hanging around the milk barn. The Timms, who crop farm and milk 80 dairy cows, have about 25 cats on their farm.

Spraying Crops

Kyle Scott of Scott Aviation sprays
a soybean field near Morris with his
Air Tractor 402A on a early summer
evening. Scott has operated the business since 1997, spraying fields for
farmers within a 100-mile range of
Morris. The plane holds 400 gallons
of crop protection product, which is
enough to cover around 80 acres.
Flying at 140 mph, he can do the job
in about 20 minutes. "It's fun and
challenging," said Scott, who spends
nearly seven days a week, April
through September, spraying fields.

Nap Time

Geoff Beranek, 13, takes a nap with his cow, Gertrude, in the cow barn at the Brown County Fair in New Ulm. Geoff had just finished grooming Gertrude and was taking a quick nap before showing in the FFA and Open classes. He won third place in the Open Class and fourth in the FFA Class in his first year of showing cows at the county fair. His parents, Gerald and Cindy, operate the rural New Ulm crop and dairy farm, which has been in the family since 1911. Geoff and his brothers, Gary and Perry, would like to take over the family farm one day.

Winding River

The sun reflects off a river winding
through the woods on a fall day in southeastern Minnesota. Minnesota has more
than 25,000 miles of rivers and streams.
It has been estimated that there are
enough rivers and streams to create one
stream so long it would wrap around the
world at the equator.

Evening Harvest

The setting sun lights up the sky as a
farmer harvests corn near Lanesboro.
Long hours in the field are the hallmark
of Minnesota farmers, particularly in
the spring and fall as they plant and
harvest their crops. But the long hours
and unstable markets have chased away
new farmers. The state was home to an
estimated 79,000 farms in 2000, down
from 89,000 in 1990.

Helping Hand

Tony Cassidy helps Loren Theel grind corn on the Luverne and Betty Theel farm near Eyota in Olmsted County. "It's hard work but I like being outside," said Cassidy, who is a family friend. Loren lives across the street, where he runs a machine shop and helps his father with the farm part-time. Luverne Theel raises cattle and grows 240 acres of corn, soybeans and peas on the Eyota farm where he was born in 1924.

Another Load

Curt Olson waits patiently as a load of freshly harvested corn is emptied from his truck on the Ortonville farm he operates with his son, Brent Olson. Curt started farming 100 acres in 1947, however the farm has been in the family since the late-1800s. Brent now runs the farm, which consists of 1,200 acres of corn, wheat and soybeans. "I guess you could say I'm retired," said Olson, "Brent keeps me just busy enough to keep me happy."

Golden Harvest

A field of soybeans shimmer
in the setting sun shortly
before being harvested on
the Charles Mortenson farm
near Kennedy in Kittson
County. The Mortensons
grow more than 3,000 acres
of wheat, soybeans, barley
and sugar beets. Charles'
sons, Jeff and Chris, plan on
taking over the farm, which
has been in the family for
more than 100 years.

Show Time

Linnea Beckel, 18, watches as her brother, Andrew, helps trim her 6-month-old heifer, Q-Millennum, in preparation for the FFA Junior Heifer competition at the Minnesota State Fair in Falcon Heights. At right is their mother, Lori Beckel, and sister, Collette Starks. Linnea and her cow took first place in their class and went on to place in the top five in the Junior Champ Class. Linnea has been involved with 4-H since she was 7, and FFA since she was 14. This was her second year competing at the State Fair. "Accomplishing goals and being rewarded" is what the children like about FFA, said Lori. "It's very challenging." The Beckels have a dairy and crop farm near Madison Lake.

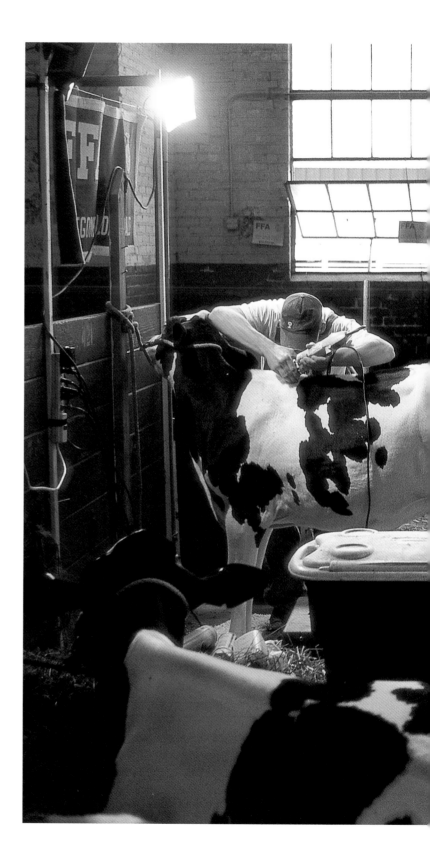

Still Standing

A 1957 McCormick Farmall 230 sits
along with a 1956 International W-400,
a Massey-Harris 101, and a Farmall
Cub, at Blank Implement in Foley. The
tractors are among more than 50 old
tractors in Dan Blank's collection.
Blank says he buys only unique models.
"I buy the ones I haven't seen before,
the ones they only made a few of."
Blank grew up on a small farm in the
area and, along with his brother, Tom,
took over his father's implement dealership in 1984. Their father, Ray Blank,
began operating the dealership in 1947.

Morning Coffee

"I'm the oldest guy in Herman and
Norcross both," announced 86-year-
old Arvid Lundgren of Norcross as he
sat drinking coffee at Denny's Cafe in
Herman early one morning. Lundgren
retired from farming in 1982 and
worked as a maintenance man for the
city of Norcross until 1997. "It was a
lot of hard work, we had to do it all
with horses back then," said Lundgren
of his life as a farmer. "We had a lot of
good times in the old days." Lundgren
bought his first tractor, an International
F12, in 1935.

Looking Contented

A farm cat soaks up the sun in the doorway of a milk barn near New Germany. Milk barns are, understandably, a favorite hangout for cats. Besides being family pets, farm cats also help to control the rodent population.

One Potato, Two

Ron Novacek inspects a load of Norland Red Potatoes on their way to a storage bin at Ryan Potato Company in East Grand Forks, where they would eventually be washed, packaged, marketed and sold. "It's pretty grueling work, but it only lasts a couple of weeks," said Ron. "Sometimes I think you've got to be partially insane to farm. It's gotta be in your blood." Ron and his brother, Paul, operate the farm, which has been in their family since the 1920s. The brothers grow sugar beets, wheat, pinto and navy beans, soybeans and potatoes.

Burnin' Wheat

Charles Mortenson burns what's left of a wheat field on the land he farms with his brother, Peter, and sons, Jeff and Chris, near Kennedy in Kittson County. The land was too soft to plow or disk because of an extremely wet season, so it had to be burned using an ATV and a propane tank. The Mortensons grow more than 3,000 acres of wheat, soybeans, barley and sugar beets. Charles' sons plan to eventually run the farm, which has been in the family for more than 100 years.

Grooming Session

Kyle Sellner, 13, combs out the tail of his 2-year-old cow, Moose, prior to competition at the Brown County Fair in New Ulm. This would be Kyle's second year showing cows at the county fair. His parents, Mike and Judy, raise dairy cattle and crops on their Sleepy Eye farm.

Gather Around

Buyers bid on farm equipment and machinery during a retirement auction on the James and Kathy Madison farm near Dalton in Ottertail County. The Madisons grew over 600 acres of crops on the farm that James' grandparents, Charles and Sofia Madison, bought in the early-1900s. "It would have been nice if it (the farm) could continue in the family, but it doesn't always work out that way," said James. "Farming was good to me," said James, who now spends a lot of time in the garden and out golfing. "But I've been too busy to miss it," he added with a chuckle.

Once Upon a Time

An old farmstead, likely built around 1900, sits abandoned along Interstate 94 in Rothsay, Ottertail County. The owner, Roald Ostlund, bought the farm and 120 acres in 1950. He farmed the land and his brother, Ole, lived there from 1952 to 1969. "It was about the coldest house in the country," said Ole. "It's not worth saving." The house caught fire in the early-1980s and has been vacant ever since.

Hay! Get a Load of This

Farmers gather around as auctioneer
C.J. Aune calls for bids on hay bales
at the Cannonball Truckstop in Cannon
Falls, Goodhue County. Aune has
presided over hay auctions the first and
third Saturday of each month since
1997. Minnesota ranks seventh in hay
production in the United States.

Corn Shocks

A field of corn shocks are covered with snow during a brisk Minnesota winter on an Amish farm near Utica in Winona County. The corn is cut with a corn-binder, then set up into shocks and left to dry until it is eventually separated and used for feed and bedding.

Braving the Weather

Amish farmer David Schmucker
unloads a buggy on his brother-in-
law's farm in rural Utica, Winona
County, on a brisk December afternoon. Rudy Gingerich had just
returned in his buggy from a school
meeting with his daughters and, despite
sub-zero temperatures, was preparing
to make a trip to a friend's house.
Schmucker and Gingerich operate
the crop and dairy farm.

Taking the Time

A Brown Swiss cow smells a thistle flower on the Joe and Donna Speltz farm just south of Utica, in Winona County. The couple milk 10 of the cows, which are becoming more popular due to higher butterfat and protein levels in their milk. Donna grew up on the Utica farm and Joe grew up just north of Altura.

Melancholy Morning

Six-year-old Ariel Way of Garfield and
his paternal grandfather, Robert Way of
Alexandria, watch as items belonging to
Ariel's maternal grandparents, James
and Kathy Madison, are sold at auction
on their farm in Dalton, Ottertail County.
The Madisons retired from farming in
1998, and with no children interested in
taking over, decided to have a retirement
sale. Robert Way lost his Missouri dairy
farm during the difficult years of the
1980s. He now works on a grain farm
in Evansville.

Haulin' Sugar Beets

Joanne Sjol drives down a rural road
with a truckload of sugar beets headed
for an American Crystal piling station
near Alvarado in Marshall County.
Joanne has worked for Robert Iverson
and his son Ron since 1974, helping to
haul beets for a few weeks each year.
"I love to be outside, it's beautiful. You
really see God's creation when you get
out to the country. I love it." said
Joanne. "It's gonna be a good crop,"
said Ron, whose father started growing
beets in 1962.

Playin' Ball

Jay Engles,17, drives to the basket as his brother, Brian,11, and sister, Lauren,13, defend during a game on the family farm in Lake Crystal, Blue Earth County. John and Donna Engles raise hogs and have 1,000 acres of corn and soybeans on the four-generation farm John's great-great-grandfather homesteaded after he moved here from Wales. Of the three children, Brian seems the most inter-ested in taking over the farm. "I think about it all the time," said Brian. Jay plans to become a pilot, and Lauren wants to be a flight attendant.

Goin' to Work

Robert Underbakke heads down a rural road in Fillmore County's Amherst Township as the evening sun lights up the dusty land. Underbakke was on his way to finish planting close to 300 acres of corn on land he farms with his son-in-law, Donald Bergey. "That's his life," said Robert's wife Donna, "He'd rather be out on the tractor than in the house. I don't think he'd live long if he slowed down or quit farming." Robert is one of many farmers who have been seriously injured by farm machinery. Although he lost his left hand in a corn chopper back in 1980, he has adapted and "can even ring hogs with one hand," said Donna.

Waiting Patiently

John Bauer basks in the late afternoon sun as his brother, Bernard, harvests soybeans on the farm where they grew up in Vermillion Township, Goodhue County. John, who was born in 1915, started helping around the farm with milk chores when he was eight. Will John ever retire? "I haven't made up my mind yet. I suppose I'll have to eventually ... but I'm not looking forward to it. If you like what you do, it doesn't seem like work. I wouldn't want to just sit around." The Bauers, along with Bernard's sons, Mike and John, raise crops and cattle.

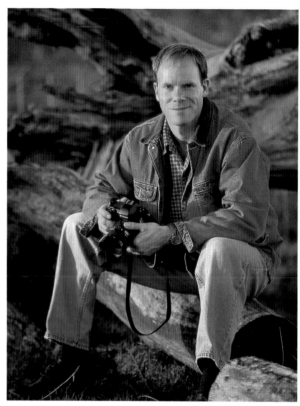

Photo by Matt Miller

Dean Riggott has worked as a professional photographer in southeastern Minnesota since 1991 when he began his career as a photojournalist for the *Post-Bulletin* and *Agri News* newspapers in Rochester. The Rochester native won dozens of awards for his work during the nine years he spent at these newspapers. Dean left his newspaper job in 1999 to devote full attention to his freelance business, Dean Riggott Photography, specializing in Rochester and agriculture photo stock, commercial, corporate, editorial, and weddings. In 1997, he published the best-selling book, *Rochester: The Images*, a pictorial featuring 70 color photographs of the city, which continues to make local bookstore best-seller lists.

Dean's work has been published by *The Wall Street Journal, The New York Times, Healthcare Finance, Successful Farming Magazine, Sierra Magazine,* Mayo Clinic, Associated Press, Bloomberg News, University of Minnesota, Rochester Art Center, Meshbesher & Spence Law Firm, and the Rochester Convention & Visitors Bureau.

Inspired by his years shooting photographs for *Agri News*, and in appreciation of the beauty and character of the land and the people he encountered, Dean decided to pursue this project. He spent years traveling the byways of rural Minnesota spending many hours and sometimes days getting to know his subjects.

He hopes his images will bring back memories to those who grew up on a farm but now live elsewhere, and inspire those who stayed closer to home.